ELIMINATING A STAGNANT LIFESTYLE
IS THE KEY TO LIVING THE LIFE OF YOUR DREAMS

BY

JACQUELINE D. HARRIS

Eliminating a Stagnant Lifestyle
Copyright @2015 Jacqueline D. Harris

ALL RIGHTS RESERVED

No portion of this publication may be reproduced, stored, in any electronic system, or transmitted in any form or by any means, electronic, mechanical, photocopy, recording, or otherwise without written permission from the author. Brief quotations may be used in literary reviews.

ISBN: 978-0-9897678-1-1

FOR INFORMATION CONTACT:
Jacqueline Harris c/o
Amargi Enterprises, LLC
amargienterprises@gmail.com

Please visit our website at
www.sacredtonemasters.com
Online ordering is available for all products.

Table of Contents

DEDICATIONS * 5

ACKNOWLEDGEMENTS * 7

PHYSICAL STAGNATION (YOUR ENEMY) * 9

MOVEMENT HEALS ALL * 16

GRATITUDE, THE FIRST STEP * 28

THE AGE OF RESPONSIBILITY * 32

CARRYING OTHERS' BURDENS * 46

MENTAL STAGNATION (YOUR ENEMY) * 54

BINDING BREEDS STAGNATION * 58

THE SPELL OF WORDS * 62

CONCLUSION * 68

ABOUT THE AUTHOR *74

DEDICATIONS

This book is dedicated to:

All women who have felt frustrated and almost gave up hope because they felt stagnant, stuck, and can't find the ability to move in their lives.

To all women carrying unrealistic hopes and burdens of others on her shoulders. The women who have given her all to others and feel as if they have not gotten anything back in return.

To the women who are suffering mentally, spiritually, and physically from ignoring their wants and needs.

I dedicate this book to you.

ACKNOWLEDGEMENTS

To The Creator of the Boundless Universe, The All, Who All Praises and Gratitude is Due. The All is, I Am, The All Can I Can, The All Does, I Do.

To El Maluk, the ruler of the Mental Reservoir, thank you for allowing me access.

To my Mother (Diamond Juanita) and my siblings, my family in Chicago, Illinois, Memphis, Tennessee, Minnesota and Florida and all of my friends all over the country. Thank you all.

I lovingly thank, Lenon Honor (and the Honor family), Don Nicoleone and the WGAG Radio family. It was/is through your positive, kind and caring words, your humor and your works, that keeps me in constant movement thus preventing me from being stagnant in my life…Ever Again.

Chapter One
Physical Stagnation (Your Enemy)

Stagnation has prevented many women from being her best. It is our enemy. Stagnation prevents our energy from flowing, produces frustration, and causes us to focus on the negativity in our lives. It prevents Divine Love from flowing within us, and, in turn, it prohibits you from allowing Divine Love to flow to others. Stagnation destroys self-love, which is needed for the wellbeing of your physical, mental, and spiritual self. Eventually, physical and mental stagnation leads to death. We must tune ourselves to things in nature such as The Lotus Flower and the Baobab Tree as examples for us.

I placed The Lotus Flower on the cover of this book because it is what we must become. The lotus symbolizes the union of Upper and Lower Egypt. But in this book, I use it to symbolize the union of our internal and external body, our mind and our body and the physical and spiritual you. The fragrance of the lotus is said by many to emit healing. It is said that the Lotus opens up each morning to greet the sun. During the course of the day, the Lotus Flower releases a sweet smelling perfume. Each evening, the Lotus Flower closes and sinks into the dark water or mud. The Lotus Flower is never stagnant and is always in constant movement, even while under the dark water or mud. This is what we must and will become again.

I mentioned the Baobab (Bey-O-Bab) Tree in the book because we must also become as a Baobab Tree. Baobab Trees are very difficult to kill. They can be Burnt, or stripped of their bark, and they will just form new bark and carry on growing. A Baobab Tree, like women, can create its own ecosystem, as it supports the life of countless creatures, from the largest of mammals to the thousands of tiny creatures. A Baobab Tree is never stagnant and is always in constant movement. This is what we must and will become again.

The love of self has been removed from many women. That lack of love for self is so far detached that many women now practice self-hate for themselves along with displaying hatred toward each other. Self-hatred is a learned behavior passed down from generation to generation. Many women ignore the gifts they have been blessed with and have given up the fight to live. When that decision is made, you become stagnant and accelerate the process of dying. Some of us look up one day and find ourselves at a standstill in our lives, wondering how we got to this point. I have been there, and in this book, I will discuss how one gets there and ways to get out of that deathtrap.

We have all seen a standing puddle of water and the debris that attaches itself to that puddle. That is what has happened to us. We are at such a low point that work must be done to remove the waste from both inside and outside of our
lives.

Our care for ourselves has gotten so bad that many black women feel guilty for putting themselves first. Women have been taught that the highest form of womanhood is to have and show great concern for others and little or no concern for your own self. We are taught to revel in the joy of loving others and made to think the worst thing we could do is to love ourselves. In fact, the black woman who puts herself first is usually vilified and called selfish. Is it not written that self-preservation is the first law of nature?

The love of self is the only way out of this mess we are in. The love of others has been so bred in black women that she struggles and feels guilty when trying to put herself first. She conceals from others her efforts to do for herself. She finds herself avoiding or even feeling ashamed of taking credit for her love of self and the positive things she is doing in her life.

We have to love ourselves, and I don't mean the hate disguised as superficial love that is prevalent and taught to us by television and other forms of media. The practice of Divine Love of Self, must first start with love of The All and end with love of The All. Love of The All includes love of self. Many of us have gotten so wrapped up in the confusions of this world that we don't know what to do. We don't know what moves to make. We don't know which way to turn. So what do we do? We do nothing; we refuse to rise like the Lotus Flower or stand strong like the Baobab Tree. Instead, we remain motionless. We become stagnant, which is defined as not flowing, not active, not changing or developing. We eventually find that being stagnant is more deadly than the false love programming. Stagnation always leads to a slow and painful death.

We don't show love for ourselves when we refuse to be active and settle for stagnation. By becoming inactive, we allow our blood to become stagnant. When the blood becomes stagnant, it does not allow the flow of oxygen, healing, and positive thoughts to all organs of the body. This causes loneliness for the organs that are connected like family and dependent on each other for survival. This may explain why many black women suffer from a deep sense of loneliness. Many of us are lonely and distant from our families, our organs, and ourselves. But, many of us suffer the most from being disconnected from ourselves. Many possess all the things this world has programmed us to believe would make us happy. Still, we are not.

Circulation of the blood to the organs is vital to receiving Divine Love and healing. If circumstances are such that you are not able to circulate with your blood relatives, remember it was said that, *"For whosoever shall do the will of my Father which is in heaven, the same is my brother, and sister, and mother." (Matthew 12:50)* So, find and define your family, and circulate amongst them in a positive, loving way. You will find it will help heal you. However, always remember you must first circulate amongst you.

Divine Love must flow just as blood must flow to heal. Blood flows as you are moving throughout your life. If it does not flow correctly, you are affected internally and externally. Internally, you experience blockages in your body and suffer from illnesses like cancer, tumors, and other diseases. Just like debris in the puddle poisons the water, these diseases prevent the healthy blood from flowing through and healing your body correctly. Externally, you have things blocking the flow of love, such as televisions, computers, certain people and other forms of communication. You have things that stagnant you and prevent you from receiving and giving love.

Let's take a look at television. Which is what we tend to do once we become stagnant. Where is the flow of love? Many people watch an exorbitant amount of television and most often see people who look like them portrayed in a negative light. They never see Divine Love of self on television and the World Wide Web. Look at some of the conversations on the computer. They are portrayed the same way as on the television…negatively. They also won't see any flowing of Divine Love. Where is it? The World Wide Web has become a place where many have chosen to circumvent the work needed to establish positive and healing person-to-person relationships and acquiesce for the ones created online. Many no longer know how to distinguish the difference. It truly is a world wide web that we appear to be trapped in. It is a place where many have established their only relationships. But, I say it is time to plug into the masterful motherboard of the source of Divine Love that was, is, and will always be.

One thing I recommend is to get your body up and start to move. Get your blood moving and feel the flow of Divine Love. It will ease the depression and reconnect you with The Source, God, Elyown Elyown El, Allah, Jehovah, Jesus, or whatever name you choose to call your creator. Let's make that the reason for moving, to start the flow of blood/ Divine Love.

Once the blood starts moving and you reconnect with Divine Love, you will feel love and want to share it with All. But…you have to move. Our organs are crying out to us for the love that is transported to them via the flow of the blood it receives from the heart. For your organs, it is the same thing as receiving a telephone call from family or friends who you love and care for, and they tell you that they love you, too. You feel that love through the telephone lines. That is how your organs feel when you get your blood moving. The organs receive messages because the blood is a transporter. Blood is love internally and you react by displaying love externally. We are living in a time where many are convinced there is no love on the planet. They will claim that the blood of others is tainted. However, you reading this book know there are some who love to take your blood/love. They know the power is in your blood/love, and they also know you are programmed not to use it for its purpose. Think of how you feel after your blood/love is removed from you. For some, it is exhausting. Think how sad, weak, disgusted you feel. For some people, they have to lay down after their blood/love is withdrawn because they don't want to be bothered with anyone. That is because they have taken some of your love/life from you, which causes your organs to react and mourn for a little while from the loss.

It is extremely important that you replenish that blood/love. You have an entire religion created and existing off the love and blood of Jesus, Isa, Tammuz, Horus, etc. They say He died on the cross and by His blood/love you are healed and saved. One is internal, while the other is external.

So, let's get up and move. Do not be afraid to show the affects of Divine Love to your organs internally and to others externally. This can be achieved by doing something as simple as walking. While walking and getting your blood circulating, love starts to flow, especially if you get the opportunity to walk outside with nature. Now, please, don't get me wrong. I am not saying you cannot experience that feeling unless you are walking outdoors. The former is just enhanced. If you are outside, you get to hear the beautiful sounds of nature. It's a good thing to experience the walk outdoors. That way, you can burn that into your subconscious so you can access those same sounds, smells, and feelings when you walk indoors. It will allow your mind to take you to some beautiful places while walking indoors.

Your only physical salvation is to "get back to nature" by worshipping, respecting, loving, adoring, and appreciating it, as nature is the true source of life. Once you have made the decision to attune yourself with nature, you will find yourself smiling and speaking to people, who will reciprocate.

Chapter Two
Movement Heals All

Movement is healing and showing gratitude to The Source of All for your body. It is also showing appreciation to your working organs. Look around. In some communities, you will see an explosion of businesses specializing in your organs. These places are popping up everywhere. They are usually in places where the movement of the people is stagnant mentally and physically. These businesses are located where people watch the most television and spend a lot of time on the computers. These businesses are in places where Divine Love is barely trickling in, and if it is, it tends to be the false love taught and adopted off of the television and computers.

These businesses can only prosper if the blood/love of the people is not moving and not showing love to the organs. Therefore, anything not receiving blood/love begins to wither away and die. Thus, the advent and explosions of these places specializing in your organs.

Once you start moving, you will see and feel the love. You will begin to once again care for your organs, which will start working together like a well-oiled machine. You will start to care for yourself and others. You will find a rippling effect that will be felt throughout the world. Yes, you do have the ability to change the world. It all starts with one person. Why not decide you will be that one. Everything starts with the first step. Make every step your first.

Even though it has become increasingly easy to become stagnant, we have to resist it and move. Love is movement; love is the unseen and the seen; love is felt; and love is touched. Just as blood, which is seen and unseen, must move, it is also felt and touched. It is no coincidence that the symbol of love is the heart; the heart feels love. Some say love strengthens the heart. It is also no coincidence that blood/love is pumped from the heart and sent throughout the body. Out of love for your organs, the heart sends blood, oxygen, love, and signals to them. You must first start by caring for one and that one is you.

It is impossible to go out into the world to care and love another if you have not taken the time to love and care for yourself. Everything starts with you. After all, you are first. No other can love you like you love yourself. We as women have gotten things turned around, and that is part of a spell we are under. (I will speak more on that later in this book.) We think we can love and be healed only by the love of another. That truly is like another person's blood entering your body and healing you. Your organs will forever reject it, seek to diminish and destroy it. Your organs want to be healed by its blood. It is just like they tell you on the airplane. You have to put your mask on first and then you can help others put on theirs.

Trying to heal others without first healing yourself is like trying to love someone else without loving yourself. Although it is tried in abundance, it cannot be done. It is a cruel trick played on you by evil ones. Trying to do this renders you incomplete and susceptible to all forms of abuse.

If you don't know Divine Love of self, how can you possible display that to the world? If you don't get the blood moving in the divine way that it is supposed to flow, how can you heal yourself? Programming and listening to the thoughts of others has taught many women to love all others except themselves. These women feel guilty whenever they do things for themselves. They exist with a huge VOID in their lives, and that void has slowly created a hole in their heart. This is not good since the heart is where love starts by pumping blood to the organs in your body.

If you look around, you will see that women are carrying more weight, more burdens, doing more for others, and receiving less love in return. Why? Because they are void in the heart, and they do *nothing* for themselves but *everything* for others. Women accept that as a positive attribute. Women are the most miserable and the most stagnant. They have decided that television or the computer will show them love. However, there is no "real" love for you on any of these mediums. In fact, black women are depicted as the lowest of the low on the planet. There is nothing shown on television or displayed on the computer that show divine love for you. Black women, you are the first who has literally become the last. I think it has a lot to do with the fact that you have decided to put yourselves last.

Women have been taught to look externally for love and think that they will feel that love internally. In actuality, the flow is the opposite. A great man said, "If you want to find the truth about anything, turn what you know around." Black women are at the bottom of the totem pole because we have practiced operating in a backwards and lazy manner. This way of operating is killing us emotionally, which is internal, and physically, which is external.

The blessed part is we can turn it around by doing something as simple as walking. Yes, you read right. I said walking. The blood starts flowing, which in turn sends healing and loving messages to your organs. Your organs will respond to that Divine Love. Your heart will feel that Divine Love doing its job of pumping blood. You will start to feel that Divine Love of self. You will start to think clearly and feel better. You will, as a friend use to say, "Step your game up." You will want to share that Divine Love with others.

If you listen to those in the media, you will hear them say the planet is being destroyed. That can only be true if you allow yourself to be destroyed. Humans have bodies that consist of all the elements of the planet. After all, it is said that God took the dirt of the planet and created humans. When you transition, it is said, "Unto the earth you will return."

The earth is in constant movement, or as you say rotation. Therefore, you must be in constant movement. The earth's movement allows for hearts to receive the divine love of the sun, moon, stars, and other galactic entities. The earth is a living, breathing, and loving entity in constant movement. Her movement allows for her continuous healing, Divine Love, and replenishing. The earth's oil is her blood. She constantly circulates it. She shows us daily how to live. We have to follow her example. We have to continue to replenish ourselves daily.

I want us to love ourselves so we can love each other. As it stands right now, love is crying out for you to activate it. We do simple and complex things that are unloving to each other, such as not speaking to each other, betraying each other, and treating each other in the worst way possible. We are so mean and harsh with each other. We show no love to each other, and many can't figure out why they are not receiving love from others.

"Love is Not Prevalent Amongst the Loveless."
"Love is in Abundance to Those Who Love Themselves."

You see if you say God is love and you are God, it becomes sinful not to love yourself…because as you love yourself, you love God. As you externalize that love, you are showing God's love. How many can say they are doing this? After having looked around and talked to a lot of women, I suspect the answer is not many. I wrote earlier that we have it backwards. We look for others to love us and make us whole, when The All has already done that. However, women are quick to say they are incomplete and looking for a partner to make them complete. The All has already made you complete. No one can complete you. We have to turn that pilot light back on that has been blown out by stagnation. So many feel incomplete and operate from that devilish thought process. That leads exactly to stagnation and illnesses. You stop living and start existing, which is equivalent to what will happen if the planet stops moving. Death.

Once you get that Divine Love flowing, you will begin to experience many benefits. One of those benefits is that you start becoming creative again. You begin to think again. The blood leaves your heart and eventually travels to the brain. The blood is vibrant, energetic, and in abundance as it moves quickly through your body. Once this happens, you will find yourself thinking faster, solving any challenges you may have, and even looking forward to future challenges. You will have energy to help others, because after helping yourself, you must help others. Because you no longer view yourself as an enemy, you will start looking at another sister as a part of The All and not your enemy. You will find yourself smiling more at others. That is a great feeling, but it pales in comparison to how it makes the person who you smile at feel.

This divine movement will put you on an entirely new vibrational level, and you will work to remain there. Yes, it takes work moving through life. Showing no love for self, going to work, coming home, veg'ing out in front of the television or computer, existing without showing any Divine Love to self, filling up with bad foods, not drinking enough water, numbing yourselves with drugs, liquor, excessive sex, and not taking time to yourself by moving that blood through the body sets one on a low vibrational level. On that low vibrational level, one will find they are consumed with death, dying, and finding eternal fairytale love instead of that high vibrational Divine Love that starts in your heart with self.

As you start to take this journey, be prepared to experience people calling you selfish when you leave that low vibrational level. Those people are normally the ones who fed off you while you were wallowing with them, and they don't want you to leave that low place while they remain there. It's true; misery really does love company.

Those who had their foot on your neck will do the most yelling and protesting when you decide to stand up. That's because they will fall off. When you start moving your blood and displaying the Divine Love, the leeches got to go. Don't be hard on yourselves when you stand up and realize that you had so many with their foot on your neck. It is okay to let them go. You have to remember how you got in that prone position to allow them to place their foot on your neck in the first place. Always remember and never forget.

Once you start the blood flowing, you will start to display Divine Love. You will also start to remember. Remembering is necessary so you don't wind up with a bunch of people's feet on your neck again. A sure way for me to fall (because that is the only way you can get your foot on my neck again) is to experience regret, feel guilt, and punish myself for past decisions. You cannot stand tall while overcome with burdens and guilt. You will begin to slump and eventually fall as a result of the mental weight of it all. Once you fall, I guarantee someone will be standing there ready to place a foot on your neck. Their goal is to keep you down with them. But, Divine Love stands you upright. A great singer by the name of Dianne Reeves said in a song, "I don't regret yesterday, because yesterday made me who I am today." So, let us do away with regrets.

We can't waste time regretting our past. Regrets cause stagnation. How? Well, when you spend time regretting your past, you find yourself living in the past constantly. Trust me when I tell you that there is no regret in movement of the blood, no regret in Divine Love. However, if you are stagnant, you will find yourself waddling in a "Could've, Would've, Should've." mindset.

You have to work toward not repeating harmful cycles. It is like a woman who constantly jumps in and out of relationships. She never takes the time to figure out why they are not working. She quickly moves from one relationship right into another. If she simply took the time to *remember*, she could become a better woman capable of making better decisions the next time.

Help me to help you. We have to do it for our sake and for our posterity. We have never been forgotten; we have just forgotten. There's a difference. We have forgotten so much: how things operate, how our bodies operate, our purpose here on the planet, what love is, how to receive and dispense love, etc.

We put ourselves under a spell of words. What do I mean by that? Well, here in America, words have multiple meanings. Under the spell of words, we have closed our eyes, heart, and mind and only utilize our hearing, which is the most misunderstood and lowest form of communication. You may think someone is telling you one thing, while in actuality they meant something totally different.

Under this spell, you don't lead; instead, you follow. When people see you are only using your sense of hearing, they feel you can be manipulated. They began to treat you as if you have no common sense. It is a sign you are stagnant in the blood movement to the organs and the display of love to yourself as well as others. It is like your other senses are suffering from blockage. We refuse to internalize what is being shown and said to us. We make the mistake of only hearing what others tell us, and people tend to tell you anything. Especially what they think you want to hear. Eventually, you will erupt in anger and portray yourself as a victim when you find out a manipulator has manipulated you.

This would never happen to you without your permission. Yes, you allow things to be done and said to you. I suppose you wanted to experience life as a *basic* woman. Well, you've had that experience. Now it's time to wake up and re-ignite usage of your higher senses. We have gone from the usage of nine senses to only using one. The nine senses are: sight (ophthalmoception), hearing (audioception), smell (olfacoception), taste (gustaoception), touch (tactioception), and the four higher senses of psychometry, intuition, telepathy, and clairvoyance. Many women only use one sense, which is hearing. Because many operate under the spell of words, it is logical that you only practice using the hearing sense. Once you have stopped using the other senses, they no longer provide you with what you need to successfully think and maneuver your way on this planet. This allows for someone else to enter your life to manipulate you and turn you into an artificial being who starts doing artificial things, enjoying the smells and taste of artificial goods, and disliking things that are real. You get the picture, right?

When your blood is not moving, you lose the desire to do anything. You take pride in doing artificial things and even smell artificial. This stems from the blockage of your senses and your blood. It also stems from allowing someone else to define who and what you are. That person will define your very well-being if you allow them to do so. Well, sisters, it is time to move. It's time to start the blood to circulating properly so you can awaken all of your other senses and put them to use. Once you accomplish this, you will not be manipulated again because you will recognize the act of manipulation and handle it accordingly.

We have to get ready. We all speak of the return of a Master/Messiah, but we have to be ready for that. There is a statement by Mother Teresa that goes, "You don't get ready and go to God. You go to God to get ready". God is everywhere, and that includes within you. God is you. God is I. God is our organs, blood, body, because *God is in The All*. We have to activate the God in us, and one way of doing that is movement and showing the Divine Love that exists within us. God is Divine Love because God is in All.

Divine Love must be activated and NOW. We spend a lot of time waiting. A prime example is waiting for someone to come along and make us better. That is not how the universe operates. In actuality, the universe has equipped you with everything you need to become better. So, operate as if you already have what you need (because you do), and watch how you start to attract what you have become and need.

Right now, many of us are angry, unforgiving, and unloving. Yet, we can't understand why we keep attracting the type of people with those same attributes. It's simple; the type of energy you put out is exactly the type of energy you get back. Life really is a boomerang effect. You have to become the change you want out of life. Allowing the Divine Love to flow from your heart through movement can do that. Get the blood moving, become less stagnant, and show the Divine Love to others just as you would like it shown to you. If you want to be surrounded by people you can trust, simply become a person others can trust. You want a person who will love you? Become a person who loves themselves. You want those people in your life who are loyal and a keeper of their word? Then become a person who is loyal and a keeper of their word.

The first step is to trust, love, and be honest, and it starts with you. You are always the barometer used to gauge how things will go with others and the type of people who will enter your life. Many of us are not honest with ourselves, so it is impossible to be honest with others. Many of us don't love ourselves, so it becomes impossible to love others. You can pretend for a little while, but eventually, the true sustenance of you will surface. So, take the time to better prepare you. That way, there will be no need to put on a façade. You will just have the duty of being your natural self, which requires no effort at all.

Chapter Three
Gratitude, The First Step

As we go through our daily lives, we are so busy focusing on what we don't have that we forget to show gratitude for the things we do have. Gratitude is a part of showing Divine Love. When you can look around each day and see the things you are grateful for having, you are showing gratitude. We live in a society that will constantly have you spending your life focused on what you don't have, if you allow it. By participating in this type of thinking, you never enjoy what you do have.

You start to feel as if you are a victim. A victim becomes a selfish being, someone who shows no love for themselves or others. Victims just wallow about in self-pity and become locked in that box. They become stagnant. I have always said you can't make someone who considers him or her self a victim happy. Why? Because the one thing they want, which is for the incident that caused them to classify themselves as victims to be undone, cannot happen. You can never do that for them. Many victims spend their lives making people pay for what someone else has done to them. Many victims become perpetrators and feel justified in that role, because after all, someone victimized them. They spend their lives angry, unhappy, and definitely ungrateful. Many don't overstand that the first step out of that box of victimhood is to be grateful and show gratitude. You cannot lie in a box of misery, anger, despair, and unhappiness and expect a loving, happy individual to enter your life and pull you out of that box. Only one thing can happen, and if you are honest with yourself, you know this is true. You will victimize that person by bombarding them with your anger, despair, and misery, which will eventually result in them exiting your life.

This will cause you to sink deeper into despair as you blame the person you attracted. You will go searching for someone else to continue this horrendous cycle. However, there is a way out.

Oh, Gratitude, The Gratitude is in the Gratitude of Your Gratitude, Oh, Gratitude.

We have to come out of the box of victimhood. The victimhood box is equivalent to a coffin. No Divine Love is in that box. There is no happiness, no joy, and no peace in it whatsoever. There is nothing you want in it. I know they say misery loves company, but it matters not how many people are around you. You are alone in your misery.

Although I'm addressing those who are in that victimhood box, I am also speaking to the ones who have worked their way out of that box. Once you've escaped, those who are still in the box will test you. Please do not feel guilty or like you're obligated to re-enter that box under the guise of helping them to get out. Most of the time it's a ploy used to get you back in the box with them. Many have made it their purpose to pull you back into the box.

As a life coach, investigator and counselor, I have met many adults who feel their parents victimized them when they were young. They have spent their lives inflicting pain on their parents, children, or anyone who enters their lives that remind them of their parents. They deny responsibility for anything in their lives because of the one incident that may have occurred some ten, twenty, thirty, forty, fifty, and even sixty years ago. It becomes a vicious cycle in that most perpetrators were once victims. But, the cycle can be broken. "Somebody has to pay for hurting me" is the mindset of the victim, and so, they set out to find someone to inflict that pain on. Yes, they seek out a scapegoat. For the ones who have gotten themselves out of victimhood, do not…I repeat, do not…allow anyone to make you their scapegoat. Be aware of those who tell you that you remind them of their mother or father, especially if they have not expressed a positive relationship with them.

I use to work at a juvenile correctional facility in Washington, DC, and I noticed many times how a youth would get along very well with an officer. Usually, it was a female youth and a female officer or a male youth and a male officer. The youth would bond with the officer, and I would hear the youth proclaim that the officer was like a mother or father to them. It became inevitable that the youth would become angry with the officer, resulting in the youth physically or verbally assaulting them. The officer would be left in a state of shock because they thought they had a positive relationship with that youth. Many adult victims behave in the same manner.

I say all of this to say that we—the ones who have made it out that box— worked extremely hard to get out, and it is a daily chore to stay out. Why? Because we live in a society that capitalizes off of victims. It's a society that gives platforms for victims to share their misery, but without any solutions for them. We are bombarded daily with invitations into their box. Recall what I said earlier about remembering? Once you're out, remember how you got in your box so that no one can use that same thing to pull you into his or hers.

The number one trick used by victims is getting you to feel sorry for them. They will have you claiming responsibility for something that happened to them before you ever met them. They will make you feel responsible for pulling them out of their own muck and mire. Do not become overly emotional and fall for that trick. The key word is 'fall', because that is exactly what will happen to you. You'll fall, and when you look up, you will find yourself in the box of victimhood with them. Remember this very important fact. When you were in your box of victimhood, there was nothing anyone could say or do to get you out, right? You had to put in the time and effort to do it yourself. So, always keep that in mind when you encounter a victim, because as soon as you slip up and forget, they got you. I know this because I've spent time in the box of victimhood.

Jacqueline D. Harris

Chapter Four
The Age of Responsibility

When you verbally pronounce gratitude for the things in your life, you know what will happen? That victim still taking up space in your life will move away from you. Looking around today, I see many victims are becoming devils. Why do I say that? Because if you listen, they feel justified in saying, "Well, someone did it to me, so I'm going to do it to someone else." Many victims become predators. Be careful, be strong, and stay out the box. You have to keep your Guard/God up at all times. Ask a boxer what happens when he/she lets their guard down. They will tell you that when you drop your guard, the opponent gets a chance to take a shot at you. Sadly, for many, that shot ends up being a knockout punch.

So, keep it moving and don't become stagnant. When I say for you to keep it moving, I am also talking about your blood flowing uninterruptedly from your heart to all of your organs, including your brain. That is Divine Love. When you encounter a victim, always guide them to a positive book, a website, a counselor, a prayer or something else you feel can help before walking away from them.

I have come across the paths of many female victims who have reined pain down on their mother, father, other family members, lovers, and friends. When those people decide they no longer want to have anything to do with them, the victims find themselves in a state of shock. As an author, life coach, and counselor, I find that the victims have put these people through pure hell, and their family and/or friends have had enough. To the victim, they feel as if they have been victimized again. This train of thought becomes another feather in their cap. You know the type. Every time the family gets together it becomes their moment to garner all of the attention. They go on and on about what the family did to them numerous years ago. The person who they accuse of having victimized them may be dead and gone, but the ones alive are going to pay. That's what I mean by they have become devils, knowingly inflicting pain on others. For your sake, keep it moving. Don't allow them to make you become stagnant like they are.

Sometimes it becomes hard for those of us out the box, but you must focus on gratitude and doing good deeds for others that empowers you. Paying for someone's groceries, feeding their parking meter, and donating money or time to a charity are a few examples of things you can do for others that will empower you.

You should be working toward or already be at a place in your life where you know what music to play to produce a certain feeling within you. A great idea is to make a playlist of songs of Gratitude that make you happy and listen to it whenever your spirit is in need of some uplifting. Sometimes you need that reprieve after talking to certain people in your lives who may drain you mentally. When you're happy and positive, happy and positive people will appear in your life.

Allow me to share this story with you. When "Happy" by Pharrell came out, I could not stand listening to that song. I would always turn it off because I was in such a rut. I had not fallen back into the box of victimhood, and I was not doing happy things nor feeling happy. So, as soon as I heard that song, I would frown and turn it off. I would also look side-eyed at those who loved the song. One day, I sat down and realized I was cheating myself when it came to showing gratitude. I was not doing happy things for others. Instead, I was doing a lot of complaining. Once I got back on top of my game, I started showing gratitude and doing good things for others. I became happy, and from that point on whenever I heard that song, I loved it. I even added it to my playlist of happy songs. When exercising, I make sure to bounce a little faster when that song comes on so I can really get the blood moving to my organs. I can now relate to the song because *I am happy*.

Trauma is something we all go through in our lives. We're actually living on a planet created for trauma. We inflict trauma on Mother Earth just by walking on her, walking on the cement poured over her to get from point A to point B. Everything is traumatic, including our conception and birth. So, it should not be a surprise when we go through some form of trauma. For some, it helps you remember. Some people only acknowledge their Creator after experiencing some form of trauma.

All traumas are not bad, but it is sorely used for the negative. Trauma is always a test. Unfortunately, many women get an incomplete in that course. And what happens when you get an incomplete in a course? That's right, you have to take the course repeatedly until you pass. Hence, the reason many of us go through the same things in life over and over again. Many of us experience trauma, but instead of working our way through it, we decide to wallow in self-pity, having a "Woe is me…how could this happen to me" attitude. We have also forgotten how we handled the trauma before and end up repeating the same mistakes. As I said earlier, we become external victims because we never wanted to experience the trauma, and instead of getting past it, many become stagnant and stay stuck in the trauma. Many never grow past the age that the trauma occurred. Physically, their bodies may have grown, but they never crossed over mentally to the age of responsibility. Or you have those who regressed back to being irresponsible.

Some cultures have age of responsibility ceremonies for their youth. There are many who accept responsibility for their lives and move past the age of responsibility successfully. Then there are others who never accept this responsibility and forever place the responsibility for their lives on the ones who they feel traumatized them.

Jacqueline D. Harris

Look around and you'll see people anywhere between the ages of fourteen and ninety-nine still blaming others for how their lives turned out. You'll see people stuck in the time and place of their traumatic event. They may have been victimized at the age of nine, but even though they are forty-nine today, they are still stuck at age nine. Some never seek entrance into the age of responsibility; they go through life making that responsibility someone else's. You know them. Some of you reading this book might even be one of those people. It's okay. Just know that you got work to do.

To identify them, they are the ones who will not think for themselves. They blame everyone else for what they do and how they feel, as if the world owes them something. All of this because of the trauma they went through. They are stagnant internally and externally. Their blood barely moves in them; thus the stoppage of Divine Love. Stagnant blood, like water when it's still, is perfect for the infestation of trash, diseases, and filth. To avoid this you have to keep moving. You can't be eleven and twelve forever…or should I say, you should not want to be eleven or twelve forever. Consider an eleven-year-old child and how they think. Now look around you at the world full of adults who have the mind of an eleven-year-old. It's sad but not a lifetime indictment. Even those who are past middle age can enter the age of responsibility. I am proud to say it is slowly but surely happening for some as I'm writing this.

Some may ask why I choose the age eleven. Well, eleven-year-old boys are not responsible for themselves. They still rely on their parents. Nothing matters to them except video games, women's breasts, and junk food. That's okay when you're eleven. However, when you're thirty, forty, or fifty and are raising your own eleven-year-old child while still only focusing on those things, there's a problem. This male never reached the age of responsibility, and if you're a woman who finds yourself in a relationship with this type of male, it's almost incestuous because you are playing the role of his mother.

Eliminating A Stagnant Lifestyle

Eleven-year-old girls, on the other hand, are consumed with living out fairytales in their head. She thinks a boy is going to enter her life and they'll live happily ever after. She is obsessed with boys, make-up, hair, nails, and growing bigger breast. Some are mean spirited and can't get along with anybody. They want to do battle with every other girl they meet. Their parents usually wind up forcing them to be nice to others. That behavior was somewhat acceptable when you were eleven years of age, but is totally unacceptable for a woman who is in her adult years. Imagine eleven-year-olds raising children. Now look around you. That is what's happening today.

Today, you have a lot of women still believing in the fairytale instead of the reality of their relationships. This is a problem for you as an adult. But, I get it. It's because you are still operating as if you're eleven years old. You did not have your rite of passage into the age of responsibility. Not someone else's rite of passage, but your own. Many women are always looking for someone to save them, when the helping hand they are looking for has been at the end of their wrist the whole time. We have to become responsible for our actions and ourselves. We can't continue to disrespect others and blame them for our behavior. Women, we have to become responsible again so we can move past eleven years old and stop relating to other women like eleven-year-olds relate to each other. We have to get along with self and kind. We need each other. Our bodies are breaking down from burdens, stagnation, and the absence of giving and receiving Divine Love.

So, having experienced trauma as a responsible adult, you need to find a way to deal with it and not be controlled by it. Nowadays, our trauma controls us. It is like a personality that has to be seen; many of us proudly wear the fact that we are controlled by our trauma like it's a badge of honor on our chest. We announce our failures to the world, but not in a healthy way. It becomes your way of seeking attention and is used to justify your irresponsibility in situations that you usually place yourselves in. You exaggerate your trauma and behave as if you're the only one who has experienced what you have gone through. Because you're not one who likes to remember, and especially regarding those things you feel have caused you to be a victim, you forget there is nothing you are going through that the next woman hasn't experienced.

Just as you have control of not becoming stagnant in life, you are responsible for the movement of blood from your heart to all of your organs. This causes the blood to flow to the brain and send messages to the other organs. This is internal Divine Love. Internal Divine Love is when your organs are working in harmony with each other and you. Thus, you begin to feel the desire to share Divine Love with others. This goes a long way to you being in harmony with nature and finding several doors opening for you. We have to do better. The conditions many of us find ourselves in today are unacceptable to each other, nature, our Creator, and definitely to ourselves. The stagnation and refusal to allow the Divine Love to flow results in an unbelievable amount of suffering, unhappiness, depression, illnesses, and addictions to legal and illegal drugs.

If you are honest with yourself, you will notice that because you have decided not to be responsible for your decisions, you have given that power and responsibility to the wrong person. In fact, your life is filled with the wrong people. People who are nothing but users surround you. Why? Because they know a person who has succumbed to being a perpetual victim is always ripe for future acts by victimizers. It is so easy to manipulate someone who behaves and thinks like an eleven-year-old; that's the reason predators are always after them. Regardless of your age, if you open your eyes, you will see predators (users) in your midst. They know exactly what to say to get out of you whatever it is they are trying to gain from you. Trust me, I know, because I once use to sit in that box. I heard the subtle words of the predator. They know how to feed your ego.

Trauma can create out-of-control egos. It becomes all about you. Remember, mentally you are eleven, so the world revolves around you. Your ego makes you feel as if you are the only one on the planet

Eliminating A Stagnant Lifestyle

who has experienced your trauma. The ego will isolate you from others. You are dying for someone to come along and help you escape out of that box. But, that's the fairytale of an eleven-year-old. You see, in reality, no one can remove you from that victimhood box…but YOU. You are the one who put yourself there, so you must be the one to remove yourself from it.

Earlier, I wrote about the senses. Once you open your ears to listen, you will hear that so many others have gone through the same thing as you have. Despite what your ego will try to have you believe, you will see that you are not alone. Your ego will have you see women who are happy and doing well, and you'll think they are that way because they didn't go through what you went through while growing up. However, if you take the time to listen, you will hear that many have gone through the same or even worse. The difference between them and you is they made it their business not to let their traumas define or control them. They took the trauma, learned from it, and moved on with their lives. They are active and not stagnant. They truly personify the old proverb "A rolling stone gathers no moss". If you listen to their story, you will begin to wonder how they were able to do it. The answer is, they became responsible. If you're serious about coming out of that box of victimhood, become responsible, and you will soon find yourself saying these eight powerful words: *"IF SHE CAN DO IT, SO CAN I."*

Take a moment to look around and you will see these types of women around you. Many of us need to look no further than our mothers, grandmothers, aunts, friends, cousins, neighbors, etc. If you listen to their story, you will learn that many of them experienced trauma, overcame it, and moved on with their lives. I am sure there's a woman in your life that has overcome all sorts of obstacles and trauma in order to move forward in life. They did not allow their trauma to control them, define them, or stop them from achieving their goals. You shouldn't either. We all have it in us to succeed.

Jacqueline D. Harris

We must decide to no longer behave like eleven-year-old girls, especially when we are grown women. We are satiated daily with images that portray us as acting juvenile. Why do I say that? Well, look at the women on television, especially the black ones, who are on these so-called reality shows, talk shows, court shows, and television series. Observe their behavior and tell me those women are not behaving as if they are eleven years old or younger.

Television is such a huge influence in a lot of women's lives. Many women pattern themselves after the women on television. They want to act like them and become them. After all, isn't that what eleven-year-old girls do, emulate what they see? Someone is making a concentrated effort to make sure black women stay stuck mentally at eleven years of age. Why? Because you are easily preyed upon.

After watching these shows and then going out into the public, I am amazed at the number of black women of all economic levels who are emulating these women on television. They mimic their style of clothing, hair, makeup, treacherous ways…the way they walk, talk, and even going as far as to undergo the plastic surgery promoted in the media. Last but certainly not least, they display an inability to get along with each other. Oh, and let's not forget their obsessive need for attention. These women wear their trauma on their chest like a badge of honor. We must rise above and reject that form of programming and propaganda. It is a *death* style, not a lifestyle.

We can do this. In fact, we *have* to do this because we are part of The All. We need each other, but first, we need to get ourselves together. Life experiences should never bring the fiber of your being to a screeching halt. We have the ability to overcome the challenges in our lives. There are millions of stories about people who have overcome their challenges. If they can do it, so can you. There is never a reason for you to quit trying, striving, caring, and living.

A great example is a blade of grass. I'm sure we have all seen that one blade of grass that somehow managed to break through concrete that had been poured on top of it. That's a blade of grass

Eliminating A Stagnant Lifestyle

that never gave up. You have to become as diligent as that blade of grass and do what appears to be the impossible in order to break through the concrete, which are your traumas and challenges. Think about it. For that blade of grass to break through layers of hardened concrete, it had to be in constant movement, a movement that is always upwards. Movement towards the sun is its goal. Find your sun and don't let any challenges, circumstances, or person stop you from breaking through your concrete. We can do this; we have to.

Another thing we need to work on is loyalty. Many of us find ourselves involved in relationships with others where there is no loyalty or the loyalty is one-sided. We have to become conscious of this and act accordingly. We have forgotten to be loyal to ourselves. What do I mean by that? Well, we made a promise to our organs to keep moving and not be stagnant so the heart can pump blood to the organs, so the organs can experience and receive Divine Love/blood from the heart. We became disloyal to the body by becoming stagnant in all aspects of our lives. We became disloyal when we try to love others without loving ourselves first. Not only is this disloyal, but it is a betrayal. How can you display Divine Love to anyone without experiencing it yourself? However, many of us think we can do it. After experiencing a lot of pain, trials, and tribulations, we find out it never works. You have to know loyalty, honesty, and love of self. Self-preservation is the first law of nature, right?

We are not doing anything to preserve ourselves, and that is leading to anger, bitterness, unhappiness, unhealthiness, and the classification of oneself as a victim. That was one of the tricks played on women. Women are supposed to sacrifice her very being for everyone except herself. For some women, the worst thing they could be called is selfish. But, you have to take care of yourself first before you attempt to take care of others. When many women do this, others call them selfish. So, she stops caring for herself just to prove she isn't selfish. Living life this way is unfulfilling and will eventually break you as a person. Living life this way also hinders the growth of those you think you are caring for. Many become dependent on others to care for them and lack the ability to do for themselves. Many women never become independent.

Mothers should create and perform an "Age of Responsibility" rite for their children when they turn thirteen or earlier if they see fit. The mother should be the only one to perform this rite with her child. Our youth have to learn responsibility for their actions and become independent. The jails and prisons are full of people who have chosen to deny any responsibility for the decisions they've made regarding their lives. And, mothers, if you find or create an "Age of Responsibility" rite, make sure to take yourself through it first. It is never too late for you to become a responsible, independent adult. By doing so, you will be able to better explain the program to your children. Our youth have to be taught how to be responsible for their actions. If not, they will not grow mentally and spiritually.

I do want to reiterate that there is a line to be drawn when it comes to responsibility. If you recall earlier in this book, I discussed the predators. Their goal is to make you feel responsible for *their* decisions made regarding *their* lives. Many of us fall for that trick, but we have to stop this destructive behavior. Elderly parents are often blamed for the horrible decisions their adult children made. They place guilt on their parents, saying things such as, "If you hadn't done this to me as a child, I would not have done this at age forty-five." How many times has the guilt been placed on you for something your adult child feels you are responsible for that happened to them during their childhood? Mothers, you cannot be responsible for your child's decision to continuously reside in that box of victimhood.

Stop blaming everything on the devil, your sex, your race, having no mother or father, or whatever other crutch you want to use to justify a decision you made. Instead, acknowledge you are responsible for "that" decision. Only then will you attempt to fix the problem. As long as it is somebody else's fault, you will remain stagnant and do nothing but place blame. That condition will have you continuously preyed upon and allow others to capitalize off of

Eliminating A Stagnant Lifestyle

you. You will never reach your full potential, but you will most surely have a broken heart. I worked as a counselor at a prison, and I can count on one hand (and still have a few fingers left) the number of inmates who took responsibility for their crimes. Many blamed their situations on the fact that they grew up fatherless or their mother worked long hours and wasn't home, or some other crutch. Please don't misinterpret me as saying those things don't matter, because they do. However, not having a father as a child should not be used as justification for the decisions you make today.

So, we can't give up. That blade of grass did not give up, and it reached its goal. Many of us have given up because things may look pretty bad, but you must never give up. You wanted to come to this planet, so stop hollering that you didn't ask to be here. That is not true. You were the one sperm that beat out the millions or billions of other sperms to make it to the egg. You didn't give up then, so don't give up now. The fact that you can look at yourself in the mirror is a testament of your divine strength and fortitude. So, as the youth say, it's time to "Boss Up".

Weakness and failure are no longer an option for us. Not that they ever were, but many of us exist as if they were an option. Those days are over. It's time to bury stagnation. In fact, when you put together your "Age of Responsibility" rite, have a memorial service for stagnation. You can do this alone or ask a few friends to join you. Have you a nice party to celebrate afterwards. But, get to work on moving the lifeblood through your body so you can experience Divine Love.

Sisters, don't think you are ever too old to have an "Age of Responsibility" rite for self. As long as you have breath you can participate in it. It is life altering and will cause quite the DNA explosion to occur. You will welcome that responsibility for self. For many, you will experience what it feels like to be a real adult, a real Goddess. After all, Psalms 82:6 says, "Is it not written in your laws, I said ye are Gods." And one thing we know is that Gods are responsible.

Jacqueline D. Harris

Gain some form of control over your decisions and your life. You can do it. Time is of the essence. Below is an example of an "Age of Responsibility for Self" that I used:

Dim the lights. Sit with your back straight and your feet firmly on the floor. Inhale deeply through your nose and exhale through your mouth nine times. Now say these words.

"On this day, I make it my intention to take full responsibility for myself, my decisions, and my actions. I overstand that I will no longer sit by and blame anybody or anything else for my actions, decisions, and words spoken to others. I send this intention statement out to the universe within and outside of myself."

Chapter Five
Carrying Others' Burdens

    We, as women, carry an exorbitant amount of burdens, and it's usually other people's burdens. We have been wrongly taught that everyone must be taken care of before you take care of yourself. I've written earlier that this way of thinking sets you up for a predator/prey relationship with others, and yes, sometimes that includes the relationship you have with your mate, children, friends, and coworkers. There's an old saying that goes, "If momma ain't happy, the entire household ain't happy." Time and time again that statement has been proven to be correct. When you look at the conditions of our homes, it is totally out of order. Patriarchy and the entire isms that come with it have destroyed our homes. Patriarchy has males believing they are the only head of the household. How does a woman give birth to someone who is to rule over her? That is not how nature operates. However, it is easy to supplant her from her position as Tribal Leader because she became stagnant, lazy, and fell…not rose…in love with her creation. She disrupted the Divine Order of things by not allowing the Divine Love to permeate her body thus allowing Divine Love to flow through the planet.

    Sisters, the planet is out of order because *you* are out of order. Remember, one rock thrown into the ocean has a ripple effect. Once the woman became lazy and stagnant, her rulership was removed and given to her creation. She abdicated her throne, role, and job…and gave it to another. She put the burden of her job on the males, who are not able to do their job and the job of a woman at the same time. Look at the males; they are breaking down from the burdens and don't have a solution as to how to fix things.

Women have stopped breeding for intelligence and now breed solely on looks and fancy talk. She has chosen to believe the lies told to her by males. Lies such as, "We will live happily every after" and "Don't worry, you won't have to work. I'll take care of you." The lies appealed to her laziness, broke her, weakened her, and caused her to become someone who is easily preyed upon. She fell in love with her creation and fell under the spell of words. What do I mean by that statement? Well, women no longer use their higher senses, such as telepathy, intuition, and intelligence to name a few. They went against these senses and chose to believe words of erotic poetry. When intuition is burning inside of her about a situation, she will still ignore it and all evidence and fall for the words instead. I mean, really, how many times do you need to hear the same lie over and over again before it hits you that it's a lie?

Now that women have lost her powers to males, he rules over her, her children, and her household with brute force. No compassion, no intellect, no fairness, just brute strength. He has written books that render women nothing but a breeder, and women uphold those books. You know you are more than a breeder; yet, you keep the lie going. Millions are trapped in a cruel web of tragedy. None of this would have happened if we had not chosen stagnation and voided Divine Love.

What a monumental price women are paying for that decision. Our homes are broken, our hearts are broken, our children reject everything, and we are in such incredible pain while carrying those burdens with us. We have now become the caretakers of our burdens, and we go out of our way to punish women who we think have decided she no longer wants to carry anyone's burdens. We are now very brutal with each other and physically assault our daughters if they show signs of not conforming to the painful, deadly status quo that her mother has given in to. The burdens become too heavy for the child, so she breaks down for several reasons. She loves her mother and wants her mother's approval. In their quest to remain under the spell, many mothers will withhold love from the child they deem the non-conformist. It becomes too much for the daughter, so she winds up conforming and the cycle continues.

The burdens are overwhelming. So, many women seek outlets to escape the pain. Many turn to alcohol, food, drugs, sex, or gambling. She soon learns that doesn't work and only brings her more burdens. Women may seek an outlet by running to the church, mosque, synagogue, or so-called conscious communities. The predators in those places are skilled enough to recognize the pain on her face. After all, his mother taught him well. So, he reels her in by weaving more spells of words on her. He knows what she needs to ease her pain. He is also aware that he can't give her what she needs. He can temporarily soothe the pain until reality sets in, though. By then, she is disgruntled and moves on to another church, organization, etc. and meets another male. Thus repeating the cycle. Many men become overwhelmed with her burdens and wind up exiting her life.

She has to realize that *she* is what she needs. She abandoned herself, and until she is reunited with herself again, the pain will continue. Women have somehow convinced themselves that a God put them here to suffer, and the more they suffer the closer they are to God. That is so far from the truth, but that goes back to responsibility again. You see if I blame God (or a devil) for my condition, it isn't on me to try and fix it. This is God's will, they will say. But, the truth of the matter is this is *your* will. You chose to become stagnant, ignore your higher senses, and are now guided by one of your lower senses, which are see, smell, touch, taste, and hear. Many women have even ignored what they see, touch, smell, and taste… only adhering to what they hear. Hence, being under the spell of words. That has reduced many women to becoming nothing more than breeders.

Many women have been trying to go outside of themselves in search of Divine Love. We live in a society that capitalizes off the stagnation of women. Everything is set up to keep the woman searching outside of herself for something or for that Divine Love. It is a well-known fact that it is within each and every one of you. It will also shock you as to how easy it is to access this Divine Love that is within you.

I have counseled many women who have spent the better part of their lives searching for "something". They have gone to many different church denominations, sects of Islam, sects of Judaism, and followed many people of the so-called conscious communities. Still, they come away with the same burdens they had before going to these different places. Many times the only thing that is lighter is their bank account.

The only place you can find you is within you. It's the one place women don't want to go, but you have to. In the Christian religion, their holy book is called the bible, and it says, *"God breathed the breath of life into man and man became a living soul."* You can take that statement to mean why would you look for God anywhere but inside of yourself.

If you are going to become a part of any organization or religion, you need to read the books pertaining to your religion. I can't tell you how many Christian, Muslim, and Judaic women I have met who have not taken the time to read the holy books. They are going into these churches, mosques, and temples and freely giving the responsibility for their souls to their pastors, imams, or rabbis without taking the time to study their holy scriptures for themselves. Many women think if they just pay their tithes, pay zakat, or participate in the patron system that they will get a one-way ticket to heaven. But, sisters, you are responsible for your soul, not your pastor, reverend, imam, or rabbi. If you studied your books, you would know you couldn't buy your way into a heaven or Jannah. As the lady says on the commercial, "That's not how any of this goes."

Sisters, I am begging you to reconnect within yourself. I am begging you to stop being stagnate and allow the divine blood to flow from your heart to your organs so you can heal and experience

Divine Love again. The hatred of self is a horribly taught phenomenal. Hatred of self also means hatred of others who are like self. Not all of us are guilty of such, but we have to be kinder to self and to each other. Everything is reciprocal. It truly is a boomerang effect because it is energy; I had to learn that lesson. You truly attract what you put out into the world. If you go about your day with a frown on your face and not speaking to others, that is what you will receive from others. Then you cry about how mean people treat you. No, they are not jealous or hating on you, as many women like to say. They are just responding to the energy you are giving to them and others. A great teacher once said, *"It is nice to be important, but it is more important to be nice."*

My desire is for us to do better by each other. I want us to care, love, and respect each other. However, none of that can happen if we don't first do better by ourselves, and we can do that by learning to care, love, and respect ourselves. Everything begins with you. Everything starts within you and works it way outside of you. Let's turn it around the right way.

It has been proven by science by the Mitochondrial DNA that the black woman was the first being on this planet. Everyone has gotten rich by taking advantage of her, like a child runs amuck in the house when mother is sick. Well, mothers/women, it is time to heal and take your rightful position as a tribal leader. "And the first shall be last and the last shall be first," is referring to you, black woman. It's time to become first again. Everything is out of order because *you* are out of order. You dropped your God/Guard and picked up someone else's God/Guard. It is time to pick your own God/Guard back up and take your place. You are the healers of the inhabitants of this planet, and that includes yourselves. You will also assist in the healing of the planet. Black women, you are planet Qi/Tiamat/Earth. As you go, she goes. As she goes, you go. You are Earth, and she is you. You are going to be the one to bring order to this planet. How, by bringing order to yourself.

Jacqueline D. Harris

Come from under the spell of words; decide that you no longer want to experience stagnation and would rather experience Divine Love for self and others. Just as it was in the beginning, make the last the first. Remove the burdens that are weighing us down spiritually, physically and mentally. Let the burdens go and let us be.

Chapter Six
Mental Stagnation (Your Enemy)

As I write about physical stagnation, we must not forget about mental stagnation, which is just as bad. In fact, it may be worse because everything starts with a thought. When speaking of allowing the blood to flow from the heart to our other organs, we sometimes forget the brain is also an organ. The brain suffers when we don't exercise it and coat it with the Divine Love released from the heart. Once the brain becomes stagnant, you become a non-thinker, and in spite of the educational level you may have obtained, it becomes of no use to you or others. You lose the ability to be rational about things. This becomes detrimental to your very being. You start to believe anything that someone tells you without investigation. Once again, this leaves you prime picking for a predator. It guarantees you that someone will come along and victimize you. Remember that everything starts in the mental before it manifests itself in the physical. Something as simple as moving your toe starts as a thought in the mental. You decide whether or not you want to move the toe. Once the decision is made, you either move your toe or you don't. Be mindful of your thoughts and exercise your brain more.

Decisions steeped in Divine Love can be a form of freedom for you. The world is overwhelmed with non-thinkers, from the least educated to the most educated. Sadly, the case with many is the more education you have, the less time you spend thinking. It's not that you can't think; it's that you choose not to. Many believe they already know everything based on their degrees. They become the ones who think and listen the least. They only think in terms of what they have been taught in school. Many are lost when a situation arises that requires them to use their brain independent of their education. Why? Because a stagnant brain is an enslaved one, which leads to a stagnant body. They become the type of person who has to be guided by someone else. They may think they are superior to the ones who they deem as less educated, but in actuality, they are one and the same. Others easily program them because they refuse to think for themselves. Both are non-thinking conformist, and by both, I mean the highly educated and the least educated. Both are programmed not to think, just recite what they have been told by others whether it is beneficial or damaging to them.

If you are a non-thinker, I can guarantee the one who is controlling your thoughts is the one benefitting from your thoughts. It is time to think for you. Right now, many thoughts are only of an animalistic and beastly nature. We have to rise above these programmed behaviors and think differently. Some people are truly blessed with a great mind. Why? They take the time to use it. They allow that Divine Love to enter their brain by way of the blood from the heart. So to those who have more education than others, stop thinking it makes you superior to the ones who have a lesser amount of education. And to those with the least amount of education, stop thinking you are inferior to those with more education. You are both equal if you are serving someone in the world that is suppressing you and your people. You are both being used as slaves of others.

So, start moving. Become the opposite of stagnation. Feel the Divine Love leave your heart. Guide it by visualizing yourself in the blood as it leaves the heart. As it flows to the organs, stop and have a talk with your organs. Ask your organs what it is you can do to help them. Flow with the blood of Divine Love and share some of that love with your lungs, kidneys, heart, stomach, and brain. Thank them for still operating after all of the damage you may have done to them over the years. Ask them what is it you can do to make things easier for them. Listen with an open heart full of love. Then make sure you honor your organs by catering to their needs. After all, your health is everything.

Many of us do not acknowledge gratitude to our organs or body parts until they start to fail us. We should *always* show love to our body. One way to do this is by doing something as simple as fast one day a week. Fasting gives our body time to rest. Most of us have been programmed to eat three meals a day plus snacks. The body never gets a chance to rest. You know what happens when you are constantly going, caring, and giving without getting the proper rest. You eventually break down physically. Of course, you have already broken down mentally since everything starts in the mind first. So, do a fast, and while fasting, listen to your organs. I guarantee you will hear them thank you for acknowledging them.

We have to break old negative habits and create new positive ones. On this plane, comfort is not good for you all the time. Comfort leads to stagnation. Many of us are in some very bad situations, but we are so brilliant that we have found comfort there. We think we should find the good in a bad situation. However, in actuality, we should do all we can to remove the bad situation. Once we find good in that bad situation, we will justify our reasoning for being comfortable and staying there. So can you see why I say comfort is not always good?

Let me share something that works for me. If something happens that saddens me, I give myself time to grieve that situation. I make sure I learn whatever lesson is meant for me to learn from it (because if you don't learn, you will experience it again), and then I move on. I have to be the same way with comfort. I have to give it a set amount of time before I move on. That's life. Life is not always good and it's not always bad, but you must be able to adjust to whatever changes come your way. That becomes extremely hard if you have become comfortable in the situation. Change is inevitable; it's going to come whether we want it to or not. Change is good; but it's something we spend a lot of time resisting. Many of us fight change with everything we have in us. You will never win against change, though. So, why not make it easy on yourself and just flow with it. You're not in control of it. My good friend and late, great author Octavia Butler wrote in her book, *Parable of the Talents,* "God is Change". Let's not fear change. Let's not become resistant to change. Let's flow with change and always be ready for whatever it brings.

Chapter Seven

Binding Breeds Stagnation

We have to remember not to bind ourselves to anyone or anything. All things are tangible and can be removed in the blink of an eye. Do not bind yourself to a person for in the blink of an eye that person could be gone. When allowing people or things to become the sole reason for your existence, you bind yourself to them and end up losing yourself. When you bind yourself to another person or an object, you start to think that person or object belongs to you. You may be the type that thinks their mate belongs to them, or maybe you're the person who binds themselves to a job, car, clothes, jewelry, etc. The prisons are filled with people who have injured or killed their mate because they felt their mate's vagina or penis belonged to them. Binding yourself to another never goes well. One always loses themselves, gives up the essence of who they are in order to become what they think their mate wants. That is dangerous, and it is always a one-sided relationship.

If I recall correctly, many religious scriptures forbid binding yourself to another, only your Creator. Yet, women and men find themselves engaging in this type of behavior all the time. Many women have defined this phenomenon as love. Binding yourself to another is not love. It is a very unhealthy attachment that sometimes becomes dangerous and leads to someone's death. Because binding yourself to another or an object is forbidden, you usually end up losing that person or object. Never become so attached to someone or

Eliminating A Stagnant Lifestyle

something that you feel you cannot live without them or it. You can't live without your Creator, The All, air, water, and things of nature that are in The All. No one or no thing should be allowed that spot. Binding breeds stagnation.

Once you bind yourself to another person, you usually cease to exist. Everything becomes about that person. You lose yourself and become stagnant. Nothing is done for you; everything is done for the person you bind yourself to. You weren't placed here for that reason. For those who follow organized religion, it should be clear why you were placed on the planet. I assure you nowhere is it written for you to bind yourself to anyone other than your Creator.

Please don't get me wrong; I am not saying two people should not get together in a relationship. What I am saying is it should never be the type of relationship where one person gives up their life and sole existence to bind to another. That is not fair to the other partner and always ends badly for the one doing the binding. The key is to enhance your partner, not burden them. No one should be solely responsible for another, and especially if that person is not responsible for himself or herself. It is truly a burden when dealing with those who have no idea what it means to be responsible for themselves. You have the makings of a tragic situation when you attempt to place responsibility for yourself onto one who feels he/she is never responsible for him/herself. It never ends well for the one who wants to bind them. In fact, their mate will eventually leave them. You will hear people who meet these type of people say things like, "They're too clingy," "They agree with everything I say," "They're moving too fast for me," or "They are asking too much of me." Always listen internally and not just externally so you can hear.

Another reason binding yourself to another person or an object never works is because you start to worship them as you would God, and I'm certain that is forbidden in every religion. No binding of partners. You will never fair well and the outcome is never good. In the school of Christianity, it says, "You should have no other gods before me. Do not make unto you any graven images." Graven is the keyword here. In the school of Islam, it says, "Allah is alone and no partner has he." There are major rules that many of us violate daily. We violate them, then sit back and get angry when that person or graven image is removed from us.

Because we have become stagnant, we don't think or hear clearly. So what do we do? You guessed it; we go and find another person or object to bind ourselves to. We put all the blame on others and not ourselves. As I wrote earlier, stagnation breeds non-thinkers who set themselves up to be preyed upon. You blame the person who walked away from you and you blame your God. You never take responsibility for your actions. You never take the time to acknowledge your role in the demise of your relationships. If you do, it is subtle. Stagnant non-thinkers will say such things as, "He/She couldn't handle all that I had to give," "I was too good to him/her," and "I gave my all to him/her and look at how he/she treated me." They speak as if giving there all to anyone other than The All wasn't the problem.

Chapter Eight
The Spell of Words

When Divine Love is denied to the body and brain, we suffer a form of mental insanity. In other words, we lose all of our common sense. You will find yourself doing things that are dangerous to you and your children, if you have any. You will do things like meet strangers off of the Internet, or move men and women into your home, placing them around your children, without doing a thorough background check on them. We are living in an extremely dangerous time, and to invite strange people into your life could cost the lives of you, your children, or both. To take in men straight out of prison could end up being a deadly mistake. To obsessively attempt to live this fairytale life thinking he's "The One" show a total lack of common sense. To pursue men or play games with them in an attempt to find out if he is "The One" could result in a loss of your finances, your heart being broken, or worse, the loss of you and/or your children's lives.

In your attempts to find "The One", you don't use your common sense. You ignore the red flags and do incredibly dangerous, unintelligent things, such as allowing him/her into your world/house after being moved by his words (or erotic poetry as I like to call it). Seldom do you bother to seek evidence of his name, birthday, credit report, why he was in prison or can't hold a job, history of mental illness, or if he has children and a relationship with his family. You check none of these things. You just feel it is your job to save him, repair him, and mold him so he will forever love you and be loyal to you. How is that working out for you, women?

I hear many women proclaiming anger with men by this statement: "How could you do this to me? I did everything for you." But, most men show you early on who they are. They can only pretend for so long before the real them surfaces. If you wouldn't be so anxious and rush into things with them, you would be able to see them for who they really are. For many women, because they ignored the signs, they end up finding out too late after their bank account has been drained, they've lost their job, or their child has been raped and molested. Sadly, sometimes the realization doesn't come until they are taking their last breath from being choked, beaten, stabbed, or shot by their Prince Charming.

To charm someone means to put a person under a spell. Remember that, ladies. Spells are easily placed on you if you do not use common sense, and please take the time to investigate, investigate, and investigate the person who is attempting to enter your world. I am still amazed at the women who refuse to wake up. Sometimes I think they can't or just refuse to break this spell. When I say spell, I'm referring to words spoken so many times that you believe they are true. Regardless of the evidence placed in your face and felt in your heart, you still believe the words. Remember, a spell has to be repeated over and over again in order to take effect. Just because a man whistles at you at a gas station, it doesn't mean a week later he should be kicked back on your couch with his feet on the table. A red flag should immediately go up if someone is standing outside a gas station whistling at you as you pull up to pump gas. What would make you begin to think he could be the one? But, that can only occur if you are stagnant, which leads to irresponsible decisions and no common sense due to lack of brain use and not establishing your worth. I remember one sister saying, "It's all your fault, women."

Divine Love will reveal your worth to you. Divine Love will show you that our worth is not to clean up behind, mold, motivate, or uphold a man. If he expresses that you should be doing these things for him, run fast! Why? Because he is looking for nothing more than to have you act as his mother. He wants you to cook, clean, clothe, comfort, and do all the things his mother did or didn't do for him when he was a youngster. The only difference is he also wants to have sex with you. You enter these relationships like a doting mother who does everything for her son. Common sense should tell you it's a recipe for disaster. It never ends well. Common sense is your protector and will guide you from ever getting into these situations, if you would only listen. Sadly, most of the time, we are so desperate for attention that we totally ignore common sense. It has gotten to the point where many say common sense isn't so common. It should be common, but sadly, it is not.

I would like to share this eye opener. I use to be a counselor at a prison in Hardwick, Georgia, and Cook County Jail in Chicago, Illinois. One thing I'm good at is listening. I would listen and learn from the inmates, who love to talk and tell everything. Don't believe me? Watch the television show *Lockup*. I would watch a particular inmate who had the gift of writing. His hustle was writing poems and love letters to the women of the other inmates for a fee. One inmate would pay him to write a letter professing his love for a woman, how a woman like her made him want to be a better man, etc. Then he would take the letter, copy it about ten times, put a different woman's name on each one, and then mail it out to those women. All he hoped for was one thirsty woman to fall for the spiel. It usually worked, because the next thing you knew, some of the women were sending him money or requesting placement on his visitation list. A lot of times the guys knew these women from the neighborhood or another inmate passed her on to another after getting what he wanted.

What always shocked me was when these women would visit and declare, how they were going to take care of the inmate while he was in jail/prison AND even after they got out. These women didn't want to listen to the common sense that I'm sure was hollering at them. They won't take the time to listen, and unfortunately, they painfully pay for it later...and sometimes in a deadly way. I mean, really, ladies. Don't be so naïve. Think about it. Prince Charming has sent you these beautifully penned love letters. However, when you meet him, he can't put two sentences together. But, I guess that's just a minor technicality as you pursue someone to take care of so that one day, he can take care of you. While you're dreaming of a future, he is only thinking in the present and getting whatever he can. You both have ulterior motives, but because you shut off that common sense, you're usually the one who gets taken. You have to turn your common sense back on and actually listen to it.

You cannot afford to live a stagnant life. It leads to a life of irresponsibility, which almost always leads to someone preying upon you. Stop it! If not for yourself, then for your children's sake, please stop it. You are not only putting yourself in danger but also your children, whom you are responsible for until they reach the age of responsibility. Stop making their homes unsafe by bringing man after man into their lives. Stop being selfish by thinking it is only about you. Stop living this dangerous death style. Stop thinking you are so incomplete that you need another to make you whole. Why not accept that you are already whole and only accept another whole being to share life with? This makes so much more sense than two incompletes coming together. Two whole beings are ahead of the game.

I remember years ago talking with one of my college professors, Dr. Joan Hill, who is now a dear friend of mine. When I asked her how she and her husband managed to stay together and be happy for so long, she responded with something so profound. She said, "We're together because we want to be together and not because we need to be." That blew my young mind at the time. You see most women I talked with were always with someone because, as they said, "I need him." So, they would try to make the man *need* her, thinking by doing so that he wouldn't leave her. However, I have also learned that you start to resent the one you need. I'm not sure women realize this. Forcing a man to need you will lead to resentment. It's only a matter of time. Society has taught him that *you* are supposed to need *him* for certain things. When the tables are turned, you will experience a full blaze of his wrath.

Women, wake up from that spell and stop being so naïve. No man is going to come along, kiss you, and the two of you ride off into the sunset to live happily ever after, and especially if you're coming as a needy dependent. You have work to do. I propose that you remove those childhood fairytales from your thinking NOW and realize they were a way to put you under a spell. Break the spell. Look at the reality and operate from that set of lens instead of the fairytale that isn't working for you. Set your boundaries and standards and stick to them.

Please stop trying to be Princess Save-A-Man. You can't save anybody but yourself, and many women aren't doing a great job of that. As I stated earlier, there is a war going on against black women, and we have to take ourselves out of the line of fire. Common sense is your weapon. Many hate us, so we must act accordingly. Remember, common sense is the key to breaking free from this spell. To activate common sense you must get that Divine Blood moving from the heart and coat your organs with it. This will activate your brain, causing your senses to become heightened. You must listen to common sense and not the words of a charmer who is only looking to prey upon you. Stop being gullible and arrogant with ignorance. Come alive, sisters!

Conclusion

As I'm sitting and writing this chapter of this book, it is raining outside. I thought of how we, as women, were always in movement. I thought of a time when we were filled with Divine Love and never stagnant. I thought of a time when we reined Maat-ly or with justice. However, somewhere along the way we decided we needed to have someone do all of the work for us. So, a being was created whose job was to toil the earth. We fell in love with that being, and instead of surrendering ourselves to The All, we surrendered ourselves to that being. That being did not want to toil the earth and decided to rule unjustly. The rein of women was over. Fairness, justice, compassion was replaced with patriarchy and all of its isms. Women surrendered her divinity, and this planet became a prison for women and her children. Women have separated themselves from themselves.

So now you are not free on this planet. The great part is you can gain back your divinity and freedom. There are some women who are going about the business of doing that right now as you're reading this. It truly is a daily grind, but we are doing it. Science has proven through Mitochondrial DNA that black women were on the planet millions of years before anyone else. However, she has chosen to end her reign, surrendering to everyone and everything that came after her. Black women and her children reap the consequences daily of her being dethroned based upon her decisions. Women, surrender only to the will of The All. Don't surrender to patriarchy, isms and all it has to bring. You are the mothers and daughters of this planet. Don't usurp the order established by The All by falling in love with a creature sent to assist you. Don't do that and not expect consequences.

I overstand in mother's house everyone gets a chance to be in charge. However, as a woman, you were not supposed to ever become stagnant and allow the house to be destroyed. And all because you fell in love. Notice the words "fell in love". Anytime you *fall* it hurts. Now, imagine this scenario. Mother steps out for a few hours and leaves you, her first-born daughter, in charge of your younger siblings. She trusts that you can do it and gives you a set of rules to follow. But, instead of being responsible, you get on the telephone or allow some other distraction to cause you to abdicate the role appointed to you as caretaker of the house. While distracted, your younger siblings are busy destroying the house, breaking your mother's valuables, destroying her furniture, and eating everything. They are even fighting each other. Imagine the horror and anger your mother will experience when she returns home and the consequences you will face. Many of us can relate to this because we have experienced it. For some of us, our reign was over. Where at one time you were the one in charge, someone now has charge over you. You have to prove your competence to Mother again. Believe me, Mother is watching and waiting.

Do you see how when you sat down and got distracted that you became stagnant? You no longer cared what your siblings were doing. Your total focus was on your distraction. You no longer cared for their well-being. So, they rebelled and tore up the house because you failed to oversee them and exact discipline. Your organs are like your siblings; they stopped doing what they are supposed to do and you entered into a state of dis-ease. All of this because you *fell* in love with your distractions and failed to perform your assigned duties. Now you have one of two things happening to you. Either an outsider is ruling over you or someone close in age to you is ruling over you. Think on that for a minute, woman.

Eliminating A Stagnant Lifestyle

Thank goodness mother/earth/nature is a compassionate being. She gives her firstborn many chances to redeem herself and reign again. The sad part is you have many women who are placed in charge of the home once again but repeat the same mistake. They are back to focusing on their distractions while Mother, who has repaired her house, finds it destroyed again. The cycle repeats itself. But, the difference is each punishment for the neglect gets harsher. There are some who are never placed in charge again.

Actually, some of Mother Nature's daughters rule over the house exactly as instructed by their mother. She does not become distracted by the telephone, television, or anything else. She reigns over her subjects, keeps Mother's house in order, and never becomes stagnant. Therefore, allowing her to receive that Divine Love. What an honor!

You always have another chance to reign again. Every day that you open your eyes is another chance to get it right. Mother gives you another chance to do better than the day before, another chance to show Mother that you are worthy to be the caretaker of her house/planet once again. So, let's do it.

Women were the caretakers of the planet until she fell in love and gave her power/reign over to another who is attempting to destroy the place. Now women sit back and complain about the job performance of the one who she put in charge, and she blames him for everything. She behaves as if her hands are clean and like she has nothing to do with the disarray of the planet. But, women, it all goes back to you because you were the first. You were equipped with everything to keep order in this house/earth.

Yet, you forget everything because you've been distracted for too long. You only use one of your lower senses and none of your higher senses, and the one sense you do use is hear. Using this sense leaves you susceptible to being placed under the spell of words spoken to you by Prince Charming, words that put you to sleep and make you forget everything. When you fall asleep, you become a forgetful being. You forgot that Mother equipped you with the necessary tools to bring yourself out of this spell. No one outside of yourself can remove you from a spell. Another Prince Charming will only cast his spell on you, turning you into his zombie.

However, women have forgotten who they are and forgotten their powers, causing immense pain on them and the planet. Pain caused by self. It truly is self-inflicted. Mother equipped you with the power of all things. So, get to work and break the spell. It can and must be done. Although many of us are lost, many of us are awakening to the spell we allowed ourselves to be placed under. We have to raise our vibrations and not dwell any lower than we may be at this moment. Movement and water is a start since it is the enemy of stagnation. We have to move because energy wants to flow. All things are energy vibrating differently. When you become stagnant, energy is blocked and stuck, which impedes you from receiving Divine Love. To unblock your stuck energy, you have to do two things and that is to walk and drink water. Yes it is that simple. You have to go within and do the work. Yes, stagnation is our enemy. So, come join me in movement.

You see, I write about this topic because I have lived it and overstand what it means to be stagnant. My energy has been blocked for a very long time. I spent a lot of years living in the box of victimhood that I created for myself. I would arrogantly and proudly lie in that box. That's how I know you are the only one who can resurrect you from the dead. Many sincere and good people entered my life and worked really hard at trying to remove me from that box, but I would not budge. I have read many self-help books, attended many lectures, and spent a lot of money trying to find the key out of the box. I was one stubborn woman. Finally, after much pain and seeing that life was continuing on whether I was in the box or not, I decided to get out.

I want you to get out now. Don't waste so much time in life like I did. You reach a point in your life where you realize you don't have as much time as you once thought you had. My lack of movement was so severe that when I finally got out the box, I looked up and down my body and found I had gained another person. Yes, I had gained that much weight. I was so numb, unhappy, and not living in *My Now* that I engaged in some severe emotional eating. I had also gained a lot of people in my life that were not good for me. I was stagnant with a capital 'S'. I kept looking outside of myself for the key to getting out of that box.

I could write another book on the journeys I've been on looking for the key. It was only after I darn near searched across the planet that it hit me. All along the key was within me. So, I unlocked that box. I am now experiencing movement in my life and feeling Divine Love for self and others. I feel at peace. Now my goal is to release that entire person that I gained while inside the box. That's going to take a lot of physical movement, a lot of walking and a lot of water. But I am ready and engaged in that challenge. I now have control of my eating, and emotions, which is a lifesaver for me.

This book is my way of sharing Divine Love with others. My goal is to get us moving so we can experience Divine Love and healing within ourselves. Then and only then can we show that Divine Love to each other. The first step starts with water and movement. Let's become like the Lotus Flower and the Baobab Tree, two of natures finest.

THE END

ABOUT THE AUTHOR

Jacqueline Harris is the daughter of Diamond and Jasper Harris, Jr. She was born and raised in Chicago, Illinois, but presently resides in Laurel, Maryland. Jacqueline is a graduate of Chicago State University. In addition to being a publisher, lecturer and life coach, she is the author of the well-loved book, *Healing and Freedom Through These Sacred Tone Masters*, which reveals her ability to overcome some of life's obstacles through her encounters, friendships, and the works of a few of the world's greatest authors and singers.

Jacqueline loves writing, music, sports, and traveling all over the country to visit museums.

Thank you for taking the time to purchase and read my thoughts.

Please visit our website at
www.sacredtonemasters.com
Online ordering is available for all products.

www.ingramcontent.com/pod-product-compliance
Lightning Source LLC
Chambersburg PA
CBHW071333190426
43193CB00041B/1768